# THE AUTOBIOGRAPHY OF BUD HUNTON

## PART 1: LOOKING BACK AT ME

Bud W. Hunton

Author's Tranquility Press
ATLANTA, GEORGIA

Copyright © 2024 by Bud W. Hunton

All rights reserved. No part of this publication may be reproduced, distributed or transmitted in any form or by any means, including photocopying, recording, or other electronic or mechanical methods, without the prior written permission of the publisher, except in the case of brief quotations embodied in critical reviews and certain other noncommercial uses permitted by copyright law. For permission requests, write to the publisher, addressed "Attention: Permissions Coordinator," at the address below.

Bud W. Hunton/Author's Tranquility Press
3800 Camp Creek Pkwy SW Bldg. 1400-116 #1255
Atlanta, GA 30331, USA
www.authorstranquilitypress.com

Ordering Information:
Quantity sales. Special discounts are available on quantity purchases by corporations, associations, and others. For details, contact the "Special Sales Department" at the address above.

The Autobiography of Bud Hunton Part 1: Looking Back at Me/Bud W. Hunton
Hardback:978-1-965463-72-7
Paperback: 978-1-965463-49-9
eBook: 978-1-965463-56-7

# Prologue

I was raised on a small five-acre farm in Ohio, living with four siblings, and separated parents. My mother Gertrude did not have any measurable skills, and my father Harry was a truck driver appearing to have lost interest in family life. Along with my three sisters and older brother Pete (Harry Jr), we lived in an older home that had once been a log cabin. The home did not have electricity, running water, or indoor plumbing. It was in this setting that brother Pete was diagnosed with Polio and was extremely sick and required an "iron lung" to survive. Unfortunately, Mom did not drive, and Dad was preoccupied with his girlfriend and Mom had to hitchhike to Lima Memorial Hospital to visit Pete. There were times when young Bud thought that he and his siblings would be placed in a foster home. Although the future did not appear to be bright, I had two close friends, Bruce and Jerry both living on nearby farms. At the age of 15, my friend Jerry Mahaffey and I hitchhiked on what was then the Dixie Highway (Route 25) from Wapakoneta, Ohio to the state of Georgia. Upon returning from my trip, I could see how my mother was very upset that I had gone missing for a few days, thus I began a lifetime journey of moving around the world experiencing several unusual and interesting events that I would eventually write about and publish.

# The Early Years 1940's

My father Harry Hunton met my name's sake Bud Goodwin in Philadelphia. Bud was hauling coal from Pennsylvania to Ohio to sell at a good price. My dad who was also a truck driver and Bud teamed up and eventually both were driving truckloads of coal to Ohio. The partnership apparently worked out and Bud invited Harry to bring his family to his place near Wapakoneta, Ohio. When I was born, Dad named me Bud after his good friend Bud Goodwin. They must have been working together in the 1930's since I was born in 1938 and was given the name Bud. Years later I would learn that the name Bud was usually only a nickname, and I started feeling cheated. Throughout my life, I have found it necessary to prove that my "real" name was Bud. When joining the Navy, obtaining a driver's license, passport or any other legal document, I had to produce my birth certificate to prove who I was, and that Bud was my real name.

# Life with the Goodwin Family

In the late 1940's the Hunton family moved from Philadelphia to a small fives acre farm, just 5 miles west of Wapakoneta, Ohio. Harry Hunton and my name sake Bud Goodwin had become friends while they were both hauling coal from Pennsylvania to Ohio. We lived there for several years and eventually went our separate ways. However, I still have good memories of my boyhood friends and adventures. Bruce Goodwin, Bud's nephew, Jerry Mahffey and I were good friends. We played sports together, roller skated, swam in the Auglaize River and went to county fairs together. My best friend was Bruce Goodwin, who would also become my "big brother" and protector. I learned how to swim when Bruce threw me off the bridge that crosses the Auglaize River. Jerry stood by as my lifeguard and issued instructions on how to "dog paddle" to stay afloat. Several years later I met Jerry while I was in the Navy on liberty in Yokosuka, Japan. Jerry was on liberty from his ship. Later while on leave from the Navy, I was told that Jerry had passed away due to a drug overdose.

Although my early memories have faded, I can still remember that the five acres consisted of two houses, a barn, a chicken coop, an outside water pump, and an outside toilet. The neighboring house is where Bud Goodwin's brother Frank (doc) Goodwin lived with his wife Althea and children Bruce, Shirley Sandy and Margaret. We were close friends and attended Moulton Elementary School in Moulton Ohio a few miles to the west on Route 33. The property between Bud and Frank's house was owned by Bud and was also used to raise a few pigs, therefore we called this the pig field when we started playing baseball in the field.

In addition to playing baseball, I learned how to handle a rifle and shotgun for hunting small game such as rabbits, squirrels, and pheasants. I would hunt on wooded property adjacent to Bud Goodwin's farm. My hunting mentor was Bruce Goodwin, who would become like my older brother through the years. We would also go roller skating on weekends in Lima and Celina Ohio.

*After retiring from the Navy, I created an event called "Family and friends reunion." I created a list of approximately 150-180 people who lived in the St. Mary's - Celina area and then organized a carry-in and reserved space at shelter house number 1 on the east bank of Grand Lake St. Mary's. These would be some of the last times spent with the Goodwins*

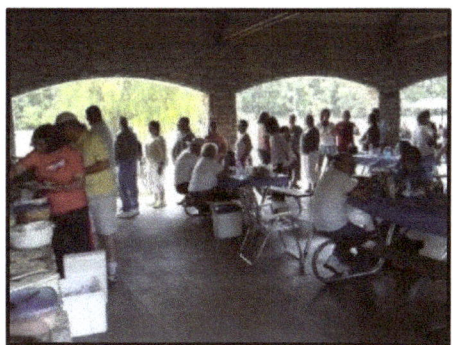

Shelter House #1

Bruce and Bud as kids.

Goodwin Family

# The early years – 1953-1955

Unfortunately, my preteen years were troublesome for both parents and eventually, they signed the papers for me to join the Navy at age 17. As a young teenager, I hitchhiked from Wapakoneta Ohio to Georgia just for the fun of it along with my friend Jerry Mahaffey. After returning to Wapak, my mom and dad decided that it would be best for me to live with Dad and Tina in Brazil, Indiana. It was at this time that I was taken to Brazil Indiana to live with my dad and his girlfriend Tina. As I grow older and drive Interstate 75 South on vacations, I often remember those days, including trips with Dad and Tina to Pennsylvania via Route 40 (*previously known as the national highway*) before it became Interstate 70 East and West. Years later I would write and publish a book titled "Homeward Bound" On the road again.

My older brother (Harry Hunton Jr.) was already living there so we became closer. We would often watch the Tonight Show with Steve Allen while having some late-night snacks. Our favorite was something called "T.V." bologna. I would eventually join the Navy in 1955. After completing basic Navy training (boot camp), I would return to Brazil to visit with family and see my girlfriend, Angie Nichols. After completing basic training. I attended Hospital Corps School where I met four young men that would affect my life. Barney, Jack, Moose and Ralph were college dropouts from the Cleveland, Ohio area. They looked after me as if I was their younger brother. This is where I would learn valuable life lessons that would stay with me forever. From 1955-1957 I would be tutored and advised by these young men from Cleveland Ohio and eventually, I would become a hospital corpsman or caregiver to many people that I would meet throughout the years. One weekend, my friends took me to the Playboy Club in Chicago. They all had alcoholic drinks except me since I was only seventeen at the time. I could only drink soda, and they would not let any of the playmates sit on my lap. I had dropped out of high school and my new friends tutored me and soon I obtained my high school G.E.D. and eventually in later years, obtained three college degrees. Write and publish nine books that reflected some of my life's experiences. The moral of this story is that young people will do better in life if they can obtain guidance at an early age. Anyone can persist in having a good life despite earlier years of poverty and uncertainty.

1955-1957 U.S. Naval Hospital Great Lakes, Illinois. Basic training (boot camp), to Hospital Corps School. Stayed at The Naval Hospital until I received orders to Yokosuka, Japan. My first military friendships began at this point in my life. There was a military draft in effect and several of my first Corpsman friends were mature college-educated men.

Looking back, I now attribute many of my personality traits to those young men. For example, when they noticed how I had my gear (Navy slang for personal belongings) stored in my assigned locker, I was given instructions on how to neatly organize all my belongings in the locker. We lived in the same barracks and shared meals in the chow hall and went on liberty together for almost two years. These college-educated men were mature and kind and will never be forgotten.

## The earlier years "on liberty"

While stationed at the Naval Hospital at Great Lakes, Illinois, 37 miles north of Chicago and 50 miles south of Milwaukee, I could easily travel to either city via the "North Shore Line" to Milwaukee or Chicago. It was an inexpensive way to travel and was convenient to the base. The main attraction to Milwaukee for young sailors was a dance hall called "The Roof." I spent many hours there on the weekends. I met and danced with many beautiful young women and then headed back to the base.

*Throughout my adult years I have experienced several unusual experiences, several of which have shaped my personality, here are a few that occurred while I was still a teenager.*

Examples:

- 1957 – At age 19, I was a ward corpsman at the U.S. Naval Hospital, Yokosuka, Japan. Apparently, someone was breaking into the hospital morgue and raping the female bodies. I was assigned a four-hour watch along with other Hospital Corpsman until the culprit was caught. Another assignment that I will never forget was being assigned to assist with handling the crew members of a Navy plane that had crashed killing all on board. I was sent to the morgue to assist with autopsies being performed.

- 1958 – U.S. Naval Hospital Yokosuka, Japan: I was assigned to assist a Corpsman working the morgue to assist in handling deceased crewmembers of a helicopter that had crashed. X-rays were taken to rule out foul play. This was my second experience, and very saddening.

- 1959 – While a student in the radiology program at the Naval Hospital in Philadelphia, I was sent to the morgue along with three other students to x-ray the bodies of several Navy crew members who had been killed when a blimp crashed at Lake Hurst, New Jersey. The blimp had attempted an instrument landing in heavy fog and collided with the side hanger. A total of eighteen men were killed during this incident. It was my third incident in dealing with dead bodies.

Eventually one of my Corps school friends, Rick Daffron came up with an idea. We went in partnership with two Air Force guys who were in the same class as us. The four of us decided to buy a used car and split the cost four ways. We then took turns using the car. It worked out well and from that point on we could expand our dating opportunities at "The Roof"

Chicago was also a great place to "pull liberty "on the weekends. There were numerous nightclubs that welcomed sailors and we were offered free rides to some of these places. In some instances, we would go to black establishments on the south side of Chicago. On one occasion as we were walking down the street to the bar, a policeman pulled up alongside us and asked if we knew where we were. He was just not used to seeing white folks in this neighborhood. We had been at this bar before and they recognized that we were just sailors looking for a good time. The music and food were good and the hospitality was great, however, I would not try that in today's environment. Late at night, there was always a large gathering of sailors at the North Shore Line boarding station in south Chicago waiting for a ride back to the base.

I remember walking to the boarding station just off State Street with several other young sailors. An older sailor was leading the way through a bunch of homeless guys looking for a handout. He told us to stay close to him as he told the homeless guys to "shove off". Then he said watch this. He threw a handful of change into the middle of State Street, which created an immediate rush of homeless guys into the middle of the Street. You could hear brakes squealing and horns honking. Our older sailor then said, ok guys, follow me.

1957 — 1959 I was assigned to the U.S. Naval Hospital Yokosuka, Japan. My two years in Japan enabled me to understand other cultures and religions. I was acquainted with several Japanese ladies who taught me etiquette and during one instance after a sleepover, I was introduced to Shinto and Buddhism, Japan's two major religions.

On weekends, I would travel with friends to Tokyo, Japan's capital city, to attend live stage shows, and spend time at the Ginza, Japan's upscale shopping area with restaurants and bars. On at least two occasions I attended a nice hotel subsidized by the military near the base of Mount Fuji. It was one of the prettiest places I can recall from my memories of Japan.

My travels throughout Japan were primarily by train. While traveling, I noticed that Japanese people loved to eat canned rice with chopsticks a trait that I was never able to accomplish. As an American, I stood out a bit taller than most Japanese. I soon learned that most Japanese people are shorter and slimmer than Americans and Europeans. I picked up the language well and could order in a restaurant or direct the cab driver to our destination. Years later while working at Sinclair College, I would use the Japanese language while doing clinicals at Good Samaritan Hospital in Dayton, Ohio. A Japanese gentleman was being x-rayed by one of my students and I assisted by giving directions to the patient during his x-rays.

The cabs were very low cost as I remember, only 70 yen (less than a dollar), they would take you anywhere in town. The barracks that we stayed in on base also had what was referred to as "house boys". These young Japanese men would clean our barracks, take care of the linen and assist us with learning the Japanese language.

On occasion, we visited their temples and I learned how to say some of their prayers. In doing so, I earned the respect of the Japanese people that I interacted with on a regular basis. While in Yokosuka, I took sailing lessons with two other corpsman that I was stationed with. It was very interesting and a lot of fun, however on one occasion, while swimming from the boat to the beach I almost drowned. The distance was much farther than I had anticipated, and I could not maintain the swim and started to sink. Fortunately, a couple of Japanese fishermen noticed my predicament and pulled me from the water and took me to the beach. I knew enough Japanese language to thank them very much for saving me.

At the end of my tour of duty, I returned to the United States via a Navy ship, USS Dixie (AD-1) and stopped in Hawaii on the way back. Along with three other sailors from the ship, we rented a car, toured the island, and spent time on the beach. It was a great time and I realized that I may never see the area again, so I tried surfboarding along with the others. I must admit it was a challenge and I am glad that I survived the experience. Two of the four sailors were able to receive their discharge papers there instead of waiting until we were stateside. We were all due for discharge from the Navy in the next few weeks.

Reflecting, I can see how Hawaii has grown, and now wonder what would have occurred if I had chosen to receive my discharge in Hawaii. The two young men who were discharged in 1959 had planned to buy surfboards and start their own business on the beach. I wonder how they have fared over the years. I arrived back in California and was then discharged from the Navy. While waiting to be processed I went to Tijuana, Mexico with other sailors from the Naval base in San Diego. There were bus trips to Tijuana, only 25 miles away from the base. In a few days, I headed back to Ohio where I looked for a job. I accepted a job in Sidney Ohio at Omar baked goods.

During this time, I stayed with Pete and Mom in Pete's trailer, located in Wapakoneta, Ohio across the street from the fairgrounds. This is where Pete would open his first gas station.

1959 – October 17th. After a short time as a civilian, Beverly and I were married in Redkey, Indiana. While employed at Omar in Sidney, I did not see a good future in this type of work, so I decided to reenlist for another four years and did so. I was then given my choice of schools and I chose the Radiology program, which was located at the U.S. Naval Hospital in Philadelphia Pennsylvania. My Radiology class consisted of four other young men. When we completed the one-year program and took the national registration exam in downtown Philadelphia.

While taking the exam, we were surprised to notice that we were the only males in the group. The room was full of young women. As young sailors In our blue navy uniforms, we stood out in the room full of ladies in white uniforms. In those days, most X-ray techs were female, however, this has changed over the years. Also, Radiology programs now run for two years instead of one. The Radiology program had a significant impact on my life, for example, I recall the time a radiologist was checking a chest x-ray I had taken of a patient. He held it up next to another patient's X-ray and pointed out that the X-ray I was showing him would diagnose the patient with lung cancer compared to another X-ray he showed me. I quit smoking the next day and that was 65 years ago.

Upon our arrival in Philadelphia, we stopped at Aunt Eleanor's (dad's sister) house. We were greeted by her husband Fred who was a truck driver and delivered beer to various locations around Philadelphia. We needed directions to the Naval Base and Fred was the guy who would know. We had dinner with them and stayed the night and headed from their home in north Philadelphia to south Philadelphia. In the years to come Bev and I would visit my aunts and uncles in north Philadelphia and on occasion, when my dad and Tina were in town and they would join us. The favorite recreation for this group was "going to the shore." My aunts and uncles along with dad and Tina would invite Bev and I to join them at Atlantic City or Ocean City, New Jersey. Oysters were the favorite food for this group. The method of eating them was known as "Clams on the half shell".

# Start of our marriage

Married at the age of twenty-one to a small-town girl with hostile brothers, my life was again jeopardized by threats of violence. My wife Beverly had four brothers who were very family-oriented and protective. When Bev and I eloped, the word from my relatives living in the area was that her brothers were out looking for me and they all owned guns, so I was a bit apprehensive. I was living in Wapakoneta, Ohio at my sister's house at the time, and this was unknown to Bev's family.

We then moved with all of our belongings to Philadelphia, where I would attend the Radiology program at the U.S. Naval Hospital, in Philadelphia. Incidentally, all our belongings fit into my 1959 Ford convertible. We now own a two-story house and rent a large storage unit.

Years later I would win the family over when I was able to contact Hospice in Lima, Ohio to get assistance for Bev's sister Ruth who had terminal lung cancer at the time. Hospice was not well known at the time, however being a healthcare worker, I was aware of what hospice could do for terminally ill patients. Ruth was Bev's closest sister and traveled with us to various duty stations. She was in the final stages of lung cancer and was living with her parents in St. Mary's. Unfortunately, space was limited so she spent her last days on the living room couch. In our current society, hospice is well known as an organization that provides care for terminally ill people.

1959 – 1963 During our first four years of marriage, we lived in south Philadelphia on McKean Street. Up It was a low-income area inhabited by mostly Italian Americans. The older couple that we rented from barely spoke English. We lived in an unfurnished second-floor apartment, just ten minutes from the hospital. We eventually moved to Tasker Housing, a low-income housing area further away from the hospital. Ruth stayed with us at this location and two other locations during our travels.

In 1964 I received orders to B School located at the Naval Hospital in Portsmouth, Virginia. B school consisted of training to serve aboard a ship that did not have a physician aboard. B school is commonly known as independent duty school. Classes were held Monday through Friday, from 0800 to 1600 for six months. Upon completion, I was able to administer first aid, set fractures, suture lacerations, and prescribe medications. In later years I would join several Facebook pages that were associated with Navy Hospital Corpsman and eventually one of my books titled *"Corpsman" America's Unsung Heroes.* Would become a best seller.

1964 – Aboard the USS Rankin (AKA-103) We were homeported in Norfolk, Virginia. The Rankin was a Tolland-class cargo ship from 1945 to 1947 and again from 1952 to 1971. She was finally sunk as an artificial reef in 1988. I served aboard the Rankin until 1966. I would serve aboard at least four other ships as a corpsman and would quickly learn about the responsibility that was expected of a Navy Corpsman. I would never overindulge in alcoholic beverages, since crew members could overindulge, get injured and need medical attention in the middle of the night. Medical attention might have been a simple ice pack or bandage, or perhaps sutures were required. *I hand to stay sober.*

While aboard the Rankin I had the privilege of meeting members of Seal Team 6. While on liberty in San Juan Puerto Rico, we had a few beers at a beer garden overlooking the harbor where the Rankin was at anchor. A few of the seals had swum to the wall area, climbed over with their gear and sat and had a few beers. On various occasions, the Rankin carried a seal team on fleet exercises and missions. Our sick bay area was often used for card games and the seals would join us for poker and other card games and some refreshments. I would assist the Navy Seals by providing any needed medical supplies for their assignment and standing in for their Corpsman when necessary.

While underway in the South Atlantic, our ship was directed to proceed to Port Au Prince Haiti to evacuate civilians during a revolution that was occurring under the rule of "Papa Doc" (Francois Duvalier) and his son "Baby Doc". I and four other crewmen went to the landing in an LCM (Landing Craft Mechanized). We were under small arms fire from the rebels while making our approach. Two of the crew received minor injuries from the ricochet of bullets. Our ship was awarded the Armed Forces Expeditionary Medal. The civilians were all safely returned to the ship and then to a port where they could seek refuge. As of September 2024, Haiti continues to experience civil unrest. A reported 20,000 to 30,000 Haitians now reside in Springfield, Ohio and are currently a topic of controversy regarding immigrants.

1966 – I received orders to Camp LeJeune, North Carolina. Training at Camp Lejeune was a location where Navy Corpsman were trained to serve with the U.S. Marines. You can read more about this in one of my bestselling books titled **"Corpsman"** America's Unsung Heroes, published and copyrighted in 2021. After completing my required training with had orders to the 2nd Marine Division, 1st Battalion, 8th Marine Regiment and medical company. Shortly after my indoctrination to this new assignment 1/8, we were sent on a med cruise. (Mediterranean cruise). The cruise should have been at least four months long; however, it was cut short when the ship was directed to return to the port of Morehead City, North Carolina. Shortly after disembarking and returning to Camp Lejeune, we were informed that our company would be shipping out to Vietnam.

The time that we spent in Jacksonville, North Carolina went by quickly. The corpsman that I met were all easy to get along with and did a great job. The Marines that we worked and trained with had a lot of respect for Corpsman and were often asked by the Marines to participate in athletic competitions and games as were known their physical abilities.

I went home and informed Bev that I was being transferred to Viet Nam along with my company of corpsman and we made plans for her to go back to Ohio with our kids while I was away. A few days later when the other Corpsman and I were loading our gear, Chief Bullard approached me and directed me to get my belongings off the truck.

Apparently, I did not have adequate sea duty time remaining to go to Viet Nam since I had already spent 18 months of sea duty aboard the USS Rankin (AKA103) before spending 18 months at Camp Lejeune and my sea duty requirement of 36 months was now complete and I was now due for shore duty rotation. I was glad to hear the news, however I could hear my fellow Corpsmen ask Chief

Bullard Why doesn't Hunton have to go? I proceeded to Battalion headquarters and picked up my orders to the U.S. Naval Hospital in Philadelphia.

1966 - **Returning to U.S. Naval Hospital, Philadelphia.** I had previously completed my first tour of duty (1959-1963). And was returning to familiar surroundings. I was assigned to the Radiology Department as a Registered Radiologic Technologist. One morning I was walking through the waiting area for wheels chairs and carts when I heard someone call my name. Walking to the cart area I barely recognized a young man that I served with at Camp Lejeune. He informed me that shortly after his medical company arrived in Viet Nam they were attacked by North Vietnamese. A satchel of explosives was thrown into their Battalion aid station killing and injuring several corpsmen. He had lost his left leg and his testicles. However, he felt lucky that he was still alive and fortunately had impregnated his wife before leaving for Viet Nam. I took note of the names he could remember and eventually found their names on the War Memorial (Wall of Names) in Washington, D.C. The Vietnam War was a very unpopular war in our country. On May 4th, 1970, members of the Ohio National Guard fired into a crowd of Kent State demonstrators, killing four and wounding nine Kent State students. This caused widespread closing of campuses throughout the country.

*The Naval Hospital in Philadelphia received bomb threats over the phone while I was on duty as Chief of the day. The F.B.I. Then became involved and recorded the calls. Eventually, the caller was caught and prosecuted. One of my duties was to raise the flag each morning and lower it in the evening. I was cautioned by the F.B.I. that snipers may be a possibility during this time. Precautions were taken to avoid anyone being shot. I was informed that the F.B.I. had anti-snipers in position for my safety.*

On April 4th, 1968, Martin Luther King was assassinated causing riots throughout the country. During the riots, one young corpsman living near us was shooting his pistol randomly into the air. Unfortunately, a woman in the neighborhood was shot and killed when this occurred, and he was formally charged. We were living in government housing just down the street from the hospital in South Philadelphia, which was already a hazardous place to live. Gangs of young men roamed the area at night, and you needed to be careful of your surroundings.

1968 We left Philadelphia in 1968 when I transferred to the USS Robert H. McCard (DD-822). The Mc Card was a destroyer homeported in Charleston South Carolina, where we lived off base in the small community of Goose Creek. It was a friendly area, however, there were a few downsides such as snakes getting into the house, and gators in the back yard to name a few. Government quarters were more accommodating and less hazardous. This tour of duty began my first interaction with federal authorities such as the F.B.I and C.I.A. While on my first Mediterranean Cruise, Chief McCook and I were instructed to pick up C.I.A agents at their homes in Naples Italy. Chief McCook and I both had top-secret clearances. As the ship's Corpsman, I had access to all medical records including the captain and the entire crew. McCook also had a top-secret clearance for his duties aboard the ship.

In Naples, When we picked up the agents, they were in Navy uniforms to avoid any suspicion of civilians boarding the ship. Chief McCook and I assisted in carrying their gear on the ship which consisted of electronic equipment that was capable of intercepting radio transmissions from Russian submarines and trawlers. In future trips, I visited Naples Italy also known as "The City of Thieves" which earned the infamous name. On one of my Med cruises, while pulling liberty in Naples, a group of sailors and I were approached by a few of the locals while strolling the area. One of them grabbed me by the wrist to show me something, however in a few seconds he had taken my watch and disappeared down the street.

Later during a North Atlantic cruise, the USS Robert H. McMcard DD 822 would actually be required to pull into a drydock in North Hampton England to repair a crack in the hull of the ship. We were taking on water below the deck and needed immediate repairs. I am not sure what caused the crack, perhaps we hit an iceberg. We spent a week in port, and I enjoyed the area, including the fish and chips. An investigation failed to reveal a specific reason for the leakage. Years later at our ship's reunions this often became a topic of conversation as we discussed the various possibilities regarding the crack in the ship's hull.

Shortly after our arrival to the Goose Creek area, I was informed by my neighbors that the F.B.I. was at their door asking questions about me. Apparently, they were doing a background check on me for security clearance.

1971 – Completed the last tour of sea duty. From 1955 until 1971 I served aboard four different Navy ships. My most interesting deployments were made to the Mediterranean Sea, the North Atlantic, Virgin Islands, Cuba and several other ports of call. I visited England, Spain, Turkey, France and Italy. I returned to U.S. Naval Hospital Philadelphia for the third and last time. I had several memories of "Philly" at this point. The ramps that extended out from the main building were still there. The ramps had always been used to care for amputees who had lost extremities in Vietnam. USNH Philadelphia was the primary care hospital for Vietnam veterans who required treatment and rehabilitation.

1974 – I was officially retired from active duty, in reserve status at this time. I accepted a position as director of Radiology for St. Francis Hospital in Cincinnati, Ohio. Within a few months, I was informed that St. Francis was going to merge with another hospital and close the facility within a few months. Fortunately, I was made aware that Grandview Hospital in Dayton was looking for an Administrative Director of Radiology, so I applied and received the job. This was my first civilian hospital after retiring and the staff were great people and will always be remembered.

1975 – I was employed as Director of Radiology for twenty years at Grandview Hospital in Dayton, Ohio and resided in Huber Heights 12 miles north of Dayton. Bev and I raised our four daughters here, eventually had 17 grandchildren and traveled with them to various sporting activities. The Department of Radiology included the Cath lab. Where pacemaker implants were performed.

At one point we were implanting pacemakers that contained plutonium (a radioactive chemical element). I was required to register and keep track of all patients who had received the "Nuclear pacemaker" I was informed by the F.B.I. that there were reports of bodies of patients who had received these implants were being exhumed (dug up) to retrieve the plutonium which was then sold at a very high price. At this point, I was required to keep the information of the implant on file and notify the F.B.I. if I lost contact with any of these patients.

# **Education**

While employed at Grandview, I began to work on my college degrees. My first was an Associate of applied Science degree from Sinclair Community College in 1979. My next degree was obtained by taking courses at Wright Patterson Air Force Base, where several classroom courses were offered for various degrees.

My second degree in 1982, was a B.S. degree in Health care management from Park University, previously known as Park College My third and final degree in 1984, was a Master of Arts degree through Central Michigan University, also at Wright Patterson A.F.B.

1996 – Retired from Grandview Hospital and was employed by Sinclair Community College for twenty years. I taught Radiology full-time and computer science courses part-time. Over the past several years. I have maintained communications with some of my students from Sinclair College and former Navy shipmates. I enjoy receiving Christmas cards and Facebook messages from them.

While teaching at Sinclair, I was asked to speak at local and state meetings on topics related to Radiology such as "Radiation "Safety, "Medical -Legal Aspects for the R.T", "Film Critiquing", and "Computer Application in Radiology". I was usually asked to speak at meetings that were organized by the O.S.R.T. (Ohio Society of Radiologic Technologists).

While employed by Sinclair College, I created some of the first online courses that were offered by Sinclair's Distant Learning Department such as RAT 250 "Quality Management In Radiology" I am proud to say that I was working on computers long before the newer technology became available.

There were no cell phones back in the day, no Facebook or any of the other social media available. My first P.C. was purchased at Radio Shack, and this was when I had to learn MS-DOS. This was very early computer technology. After retiring from Sinclair College, I began my writing career. While home on leave in the Navy, I would often tell my relatives about some of my adventures and frequently was told, "You should write about that."

I started taking notes and before long I was writing my first book. In 2019 I wrote *Leaving Home* and *Navy Blue*. At the time of this writing, I am now writing *Leaving Home II – Coming of Age in the Navy*.

Although Distant Learning was a very welcome technology, eventually this technology would create changes in the Educational Landscape. In the year 2024, Sinclair announced plans to close two of its satellite learning centers that had been open for 18 years. One in Englewood and another in Huber Heights. I previously taught at both locations in addition to teaching on the main campus.

The reason given for closing was due to low enrollment. In my opinion, the ability of students to use computers and take courses online was the most influential occurrence that created this change. Looking forward, I can see that Artificial Intelligence will also make changes in the future of education.

During my time at Sinclair, I served on several professional committees and was a member of organizations such as:

- American Registry of Radiologic Technologist
- American Society of Radiologic Technologist
- Ohio Society of Radiologic Technologist
- Greater Dayton Medical Imaging Association (president)

Now that Sinclair has closed the Distant Learning Center in Huber Heights, the space will be used for the Huber Heights Senior Center, which has hundreds of members and will find this space very beneficial. Early in my career as an author, I published numerous articles in Advance Magazine such as "Current Concepts in Radiology Management" and "Facilities Project Management"

Classroom courses taught at Sinclair College included:

- HIM 121 Basic Medical Terminology
- HIM 122 Specialized Medical Terminology
- ALH 105 Introduction to Allied Health
- ALH 121 Allied Health Management
- ALH 103 Introduction to Health Care Delivery
- RAT 265 Radiation Protection for the General Machine Operator

- RAT 265 Principles of X-ray Technique
- RAT 250 Quality Management in Radiology

In addition to classroom courses, I taught several online courses. During the summer quarter, I opted to do only online courses which permitted Bev and I to travel to a condo in Florida where I was able to teach via my laptop P.C. We usually went to Navarre Beach Florida, located in the Northwest panhandle of Florida. From Navarre Beach, it was a short drive to the Naval Air Station in Pensacola Florida. The Naval base was also the home for the Navy's Blue Angels, our favorite air team that appeared in the Dayton Air Show.

Navarre Beach Florida was also the home of my cousin Carole Cigich, her husband Ed and Carole's mother. When Ed and Carole's mother both passed, Carole moved on to various locations throughout the U.S. and ended up in Pennsylvania with other relatives. I was in contact with Carole by phone for a few years and have not heard from her in the past year or so.

# Vacation Time

Our vacations were numerous and enjoyable. Although I am unable to remember all our vacations, here are a few highlights:

**Las Vegas, Nevada** — Flew to Vegas on three different occasions. Did some gambling, and took in some great shows including Wayne Newton and a few other celebrities. On one visit we rented a car and drove to Hoover Dam. Very interesting trip.

**Grand Canyon** — went to Grand Canyon via railroad train. Very interesting and entertaining. There were country musicians on the train who played music from the base hotel up to the point of entry. Took good pictures.

**Niagara Falls** — Drove from Ohio and visited the falls on the Canadian side. Breath-taking view. Interesting drive through the area.

**Myrtle Beach, South Carolina** — Enjoyed the beautiful beaches. Bev and I drove to the area and stayed for five days.

**Jacksonville** — Florida. Attended a Navy reunion and enjoyed the beach area.

Branson, Missouri – Attended the Navy reunion for one visit and went on our own for a second visit. We have visited Disneyland Amusement Park twice with family, Kings Island and several other amusement parks. Several of our out-of-state trips were made to attend organized sporting games with our grandkids.

# About my relatives

Harry Hunton Jr. my brother also known as Pete, was the oldest of my siblings. Pete and Bonnie had one child named Randy. Margaret Hunton (Poppe) was the next oldest after Pete. Pete passed away several years ago due to medical complications related to multiple medical conditions. Margaret, known as Aggie passed away on September 11th, 2024 at the age of 88. I Was the next child followed by Sarah (Sally) Hunton. Sally was married to at least five different men that I can recall. Jackie Hunton was the youngest of the Hunton siblings and only had three husbands that I can remember.

Pete and I lived with Dad and his common-law wife Tina Rogers in Brazil, Indiana around 1952. Pete's real name was Harry P. Hunton Jr., which in fact created a problem for Dad. Apparently, our father Harry Hunton had not been paying income tax, even though he was working full-time as a truck driver. The IRS noticed that my brother Harry P. Hunton Jr. was paying taxes, so obviously they figured out that Harry Hunton senior was not paying his fair share of taxes and acted. Dad was required to pay the back taxes in payments. In 2023, I wrote book number 7, "The Life of Harry" one of my funniest books and best sellers. This book depicts my dad's life and some very unusual events. One of my best sellers to date.

Eventually, Pete moved back to our hometown of Wapakoneta, Ohio where he managed a gas station with his wife Bonny. I stayed a while longer and eventually joined the Navy at age 17. On my weekend off I would often travel back to Ohio via train from Chicago to Lima, where my sister Aggie would pick me up at the train station. I would alternate between visits to Wapakoneta, Ohio and Brazil Indiana on my weekends off. My primary reason for going to Brazil Indiana was to see Dad and my girlfriend Angie Nichols. Some of my weekends were spent with my Navy buddies hanging out at the base or going into Chicago to visit various bars and nightclubs. I have mentioned my experience regarding this matter in some of my books.

# Travel time

As previously mentioned, In the year 2022, I wrote and published a book titled "Homeward Bound". This book also reflected my experience while living in Huber Heights, Ohio for fifty years. Our home was just south of Interstate Route 70 and a few miles east of Interstate 75.

Bev and I would frequently travel with family or take trips on our own to several locations including Indiana, Illinois, Tennessee, Nevada, Arizona, North and South Carolina, Virginia, West Virginia, North Dakota, and Florida. This book also included the history of our highways and transportation. Several colored photographs are included in the book to illustrate the beauty of our country. This book along with nine others is available through my website: www.budhuntonsbooks.com. Some of our favorite vacations include Las Vegas, the Grand Canyon, and Niagara Falls. In addition to our vacations, Bev and I have often traveled to various states to attend sports events with our grandchildren. Most of these states have been along the east coast down to and including Florida.

# Navy cruises

During my twenty years in the Navy, I cruised the Mediterranean Sea several times on various ships, the Virgin Islands, and The Caribbean Sea, including Cuba, Jamaica and other ports of call in the region. I was able to visit France, Italy, Greece and Spain during my cruises. Spent time in North Hampton, England while the USS Robert H. McCard was in drydock for repairs for seven days. The dry dock in England was where the ship was placed after striking ice in the North Atlantic. We took on water in the forward engine room and although we were not in any danger of sinking, repairs had to be made. The North Atlantic has a beauty of its own. We could see the northern lights at night, and it was quite a show. This is also known as Aurora borealis. While cruising off the coast of North Africa, I could see sandstorms blowing wildly. While refueling in North Africa, A few of us paid to take a ride on a camel.

Farther south of the Atlantic, My ships have been to Cuba, Puerto Rico, and the Virgin Islands. The crew loved to swim from the beaches and sometimes from the side of the ship, although this was more hazardous than the beach area. When the "swim call" was announced, the captain was permitting for all hands to take a dip in the warm waters. When this occurred, there were sailors with rifles standing by just in case sharks appeared.

While in the Mediterranean we visited Spain and the port of Palma where the McCard Chiefs had a favorite bar. While in the port of Monaco France, Princess Grace Kelly came aboard for the change of command ceremony for Captain Brown, our ship captain. While off the coast of Italy, a shipmate received a broken jaw after getting into got into a fight aboard a ship and I had to evacuate him to a British hospital in Malta, via a ferry boat. It was a very interesting trip and was very unusual as well. We were both in uniform and civilians were asking us where we came from. Our consultation with the British naval surgeon went well and no further treatment was necessary.

Countries and Islands visited in 20 years:

- Japan
- England
- Monaco France
- Greece
- Turkey
- Italy
- Spain
- Virgin Islands (St. Croix, St. Thomas, Frederiksted)
- Puerto Rico
- Cuba
- North Africa (Tunisa, Morocco)

# Looking back

My worldwide experiences have shaped my ideas and personality. I am very cautious where I take my family for dinner or social events of any type. Although the world is still a beautiful place, I see and hear about violence daily. Mass shootings are very common, and prisons are now full of lawbreakers. In restaurants, I have developed a habit of sitting at a table so I can see who is coming in the door, in other words, always be prepared for violence. Whenever our ship pulled into a port of call, the crew was always informed of places to stay away from, and what type of actions or behavior could get you arrested by the local authorities.

In our current society, it has become acceptable in some cities for partygoers to carry their drink from one bar to the other, even while inebriated. My observation has been that this is a problem waiting to happen. As a former sailor who has traveled the world, I can see that there are consequences to permissiveness when it comes to alcoholic beverages. I have avoided crowded areas ever since Covid, and in today's scenario of mass shootings, I have another reason to avoid crowded areas. This may sound like I am being a bit overly concerned for safety, however since I have survived for the last 86 years and lived to write about it, my instincts cannot be that far off.

As a young man traveling the world, I have seen some amazing changes to our cultures and laws. Since retiring from the Navy and moving back to Ohio about fifty years ago, traffic on the roads has changed. The house that Bev and I raised our children in has grown with remodeling efforts and increased appearances. We purchased this house for $37, 000. and it is now worth well over $200,000.00. At one time there was a farm just down the road from us that had horses in their meadow. They rode the horses daily past our house. Now in 2024, this same road (Taylorsville, Road) is heavy with traffic and several accidents have occurred involving speeding vehicles.

In today's setting the same road (Taylorsville Road), is an extremely busy highway with frequent accidents occurring. The accident rate for motor vehicles has increased in most parts of the country for several reasons. There has been a huge increase in traffic since it is now easier to access ownership of vehicles. Part of this is due to leasing programs and low financing.

My home area is located just north of Dayton, Ohio. Interstate 75 is just to our west and runs north and south. Interstate 70 is just to our north and runs east and west. According to a national broadcasting announcement months ago, this area has the highest accident kill rate in the country. Much of this is attributed to drinking while driving. No big surprise there. Unfortunately, As of August 6$^{th}$, 2024, recreational marijuana has been approved for the state of Ohio. The outcome of this will only see the number of accidents and deaths increase.

## Looking back – Summary.

Marijuana, pot, weed, or whatever you choose to call it is your choice. Please keep in mind that even though it is legal, overuse while driving can have severe consequences. Also, the news media is reminding us that employers may still fire you if you fail a drug screen test. Companies are not required to ignore marijuana on drug tests and marijuana stays in your system much longer than alcohol. My only experience with marijuana was in 1957 while I was stationed at the Naval Hospital in Yokosuka, Japan. Several of the downtown bars permitted smoking, including marijuana. Personally, I did not like the smell of it, so I avoided those bars.

## Why do I write books?

I have often been asked this question and here is my answer: Several times when I was home on leave from the Navy, I would be telling my friends and relatives about my deployment adventures in foreign countries, and I would hear "you should write about that". Long story short I began writing about my various experiences and then doing research on various topics that related to my stories. Long story short, this is my legacy,

Having retired from the Navy and eventually teaching computer technology at Sinclair Community College in Dayton, Ohio contributed to my success as a writer. Regarding computer technology, my first computer came from Radio Shack in 1977. It was the TR model 80 that sold for $399.00. Keep in mind that the Windows app did not exist at that time. Before the widespread adoption of Graphical user interfaces (GUIs), people interacted with computers primarily through text-based interfaces. In other words, all commands had to be typed in.

I brought my TR 80 to work with me at Grandview Hospital and used it for administrative purposes and accounting. After leaving Grandview and teaching at Sinclair College, the technology had advanced, and I was one of the first instructors to use the new technology. With these acquired PC skills, I was asked by the Sinclair Administration to do some of the first online courses. I was very happy to do this and enjoyed the work. I was amazed that several students from out of state had enrolled in my online courses.

## Healthcare issues

Since retiring from the Navy in 1975, I have encountered several medical issues. Fortunately, my medical knowledge as a Navy Hospital Corpsman has assisted me in understanding and treating my ailments. At age 86 I have dealt with the following:

- Diabetes
- Hypertension
- Arthritis, gout
- Prostate enlargement
- Iron deficiency

- Skin cancer (Multiple issues with surgical removal)
- August 2024 - Bev and I both had Covid 19

Fortunately, my training and background as a Navy Hospital Corpsman have assisted me in most medical matters during my lifetime.

I currently take nine medications daily, plus vitamins and fish oil to assist with my healthcare. Fortunately, I only live 20 minutes away from Wright Patterson Airforce Base, so I can receive healthcare and medications at no cost. Bev also receives the same benefits as the spouse of a military retiree. When our kids were younger they also received benefits from the base hospital. I quit smoking back in 1959 when I was training to become a Radiologic Technologist at the Naval Hospital in Philadelphia. I was checking a chest x-ray that I had taken by placing it on the viewing box. A radiologist standing next to me pointed out that it was obvious that his patient had lung cancer. He then proceeded to show me another patient's chest x-ray and pointed out the differences between the two films.

He also commented that this particular patient did not have long to live. It was at this point that I quit smoking. I was not a heavy smoker, however, I felt that that this was a heads-up warning for me. During my retirement years, I have used several methods of keeping physically fit including long walks at the flea market, and physical therapy for multiple reasons such as balance and flexibility.

## Current activity

In addition to writing books, I am engaged in Facebook activities with approximately 180 fb friends. I have multiple fb pages such as Corpsman (5 different versions) and staying in touch with friends and acquaintances. Some of my books such as "CORPSMAN" America's Unsung Heroes, have done well online.

I use my FB page to advertise and promote changes or additions to my publishing status. I always have my cell phone with me no matter where I go. I get constant messages and updates on the phone. My newest car is a 2024 Chevvy Blazer which charges my phone when I lay it on the area in front of the gearshift, no plug-in is required. My first car was a 1948 Chev, convertible, then in 1959 a Ford Fairlane convertible when Bev and I got married.

## History of Huber Heights *(Bev and I raised four daughters and several grandchildren here)*

The history of Huber Heights as a community is largely shaped by its history. It is also to the past that we must look to identify those elements, events, and attitudes that will serve as the foundation for further defining the City's image. Wayne Township is named in honor of Major General Anthony Wayne. George Washington named him Commander-in-Chief of the United States Army in April of 1792. He was probably best known in this part of the country for his decisive victory at the Battle of Fallen Timbers, what is now Toledo, Ohio. Our daughters attended Wayne High School in Huber Heights. Interstate 70 east and west is just north of our home of 50 years. Interstate 75 north and south lies just to the west of our home. This area is approximately fifty miles south of the hometowns of St. Mary's and Wapakoneta.

Wayne Township, formed January 1, 1810, occupies the northeastern corner of Montgomery County. It joins Miami County on the north and Clark and Greene Counties on the east with Greene County also being a part of the southern border.

The first township election was held at the house of Benjamin Van Cleve on Stauton Road on January 20, 1810. In 1917-18, the Wayne Township Centralized School was built on the site of what today is Titus Elementary School. In 1946 the first firehouse was built in the township located in what is today the Miami Villa Plat. By 1950, the population of the township was estimated at 1,921 persons.

## Development of Huber Heights

The 1990s brought a surge in commercial and industrial development around the various residential plats. The North Heights Plaza and North Park Center brought numerous retail and commercial establishments that expanded the shopping opportunities for the residents. 1994 brought the development of Center Point 70 Commerce Park. Between 1994 and 1998, over 15 manufacturing businesses opened, employing over 1,700 people. In 1998, close to 700 businesses were established in Huber Heights.

From 1998 to 2004, Executive Blvd. was expanded from Old Troy Pike to Brandt Pike bringing in FedEx and Yellow Freights along with other transportation and manufacturing companies. Coca-Cola is located north of Interstate 70 opening another commercial area on Coca-Cola Way. The first phase of the Carriage Trails Community broke ground in November 2003 and there are plans for a future school and fire station in that community. In 2005 The Oaks of Huber Heights and Artisans Walk began building and the Huber Heights YMCA opened its doors as the newest addition to the City of Huber Heights.

### About the Huber Heights Senior Center

Bev and I joined the Huber Heights Senior Center in June of 2024. We usually attend a couple of times a week for bingo and other activities. We have met some very nice people at the center, which was originated in 1991. Prior to that year, a schoolhouse in Huber Heights was the meeting place for seniors. A monthly

Newsletter and schedule is provided for all members. Bev and I usually attend bingo on Tuesdays. The games last for a few hours and allow us to get out and interact with other seniors. We also participate in events such as buffet dinners with entertainment. Several other activities are offered such as exercising, and games. Dancing etc. The center serves the community well.

# Photos from the Senior Center

Geneva, Carolyn Joy and Jan

Jim Docker

Betty

Paul

Tom

Ruthie

Jan Weller

Judy

# Huber Heights Senior Center

Chambersburg Road

Book Winner
Mary Jane Stidham

Kati Durst and Pat Lokai

Jan Wishon

Judy Blankenship

Book Winner

Veterans Day at the Senior Center

Sister's Playing Bingo

In June 2024, I wrote and published book number 8, "Israel and Hamas at War" The world reacts. It was a challenge to write this book since there were so many books about this war already being published. I personally contacted the copyright office and had the book registered. My book is now officially registered with the Library of Congress, United States Copyright Office in Washington, D.C.

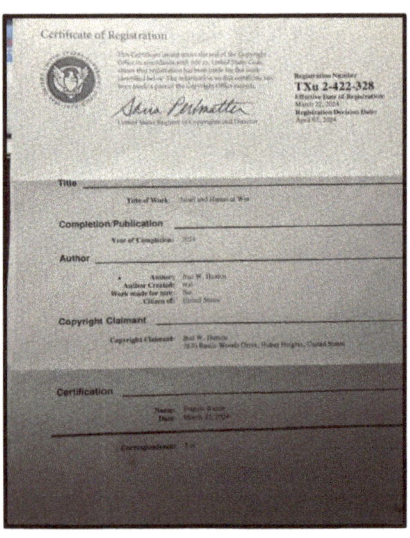

# Family Pictures

Bev 18 years old and Bud 21

Makley family at Rustic Haven

Four of our grandkids L-R: Brandon, Beanna, Troy and Dylan

Hunton kids with Dad Harry

Mother's Day 2023

# Photos of my Assignments

U.S.N.H. Phila. 1959-1963

I was assigned to the Naval Hospital Philadelphia three different times. The hospital was officially closed in 1988 and demolished shortly afterwards.

U.S.N.H.
Yokosuka, Japan
1957-1959

USS Rankin (AKA – 103)

LCM used to evacuate civilians from Haiti

Mount Fuji, Japan

USS Robert H McCard DD-822 1968-1971

Camp Lejune N.C. 1965

Sinclair Community College,
Dayton, Ohio

Grandview aHospital
Dayton, Oio

# Through The Years

1955; 19 years old

1971; 34 years old

In my 40's

In my 70's

In my 80's at the Seniors Center

Printed in the USA
CPSIA information can be obtained
at www.ICGtesting.com
LVHW060616261124
797245LV00019B/342